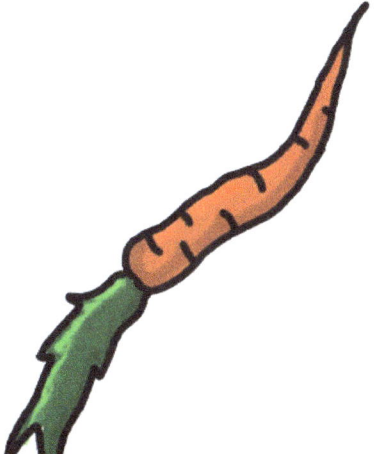

**Published Worldwide by
The Rusty Publishing Company
1st Printing**

For information email rustyaustin@gmail.com

Special Thanks to Lu Serra

The Carrot Is Orange

by Rusty Austin
Illustrated by Graham Henderson

For Carlo
I love you more than food!

TABLE OF FOOD

Carrot ...
Bacon ...
Breakfast ...
Cottage Cheese ...
Oatmeal ...
Orange Juice ...
Glazed Donuts ...
Chocolate Ice Cream ...
Celery ...
P B and J ...
Chocolate Chip Cookie ...
Chiliburger ...
Mayonnaise ...
Tacos ...
Pepperoni Pizza ...
Fruit ...
Twinkie ...
Burrito ...

Chocolate Milkshake ...
Fried Chicken ...
Risotto ...
Steak ...
Potato ...
Carne Asada ...
Onion Soup ...
Hot Fudge Sundae ...
Spaghetti ...
Cereal ...
Brownies ...
Prime Rib ...
Hot Chocolate ...
DO IT YOURSELF:
Bologna Sandwich ...
Mac and Cheese ...
Popsicle ...
Watermelon ...

The Carrot is orange
sweet and crunchy
and you should eat one
if you feel munchy

The tastiest morsel
is the last piece of Bacon
I cannot deny
for Bacon I'm achin'

Fried Eggs, Bacon,
Hash Browns, Toast,
Cup of Coffee refilled
it's simply the most

Cottage Cheese and Blueberries
juicy and sweet
that's a breakfast
that's good to eat

Oatmeal and Brown Sugar
will start you off right
it sticks to your ribs
all day and all night

Orange Juice squeezed fresh
is super yummy
especially when
it's in my tummy

Give me a Glazed Donut
any day
in fact I'll take two
and be on my way

Oh how I dream
of Chocolate Ice Cream
breakfast, lunch, or dinner
it's always a winner

The Celery Stick
is lonely and green
but add Peanut Butter
and it's lean and mean

A Peanut Butter and Jelly
with Potato Chips
is the perfect lunch
at home or on trips

A Chocolate Chip Cookie
fresh out of the oven
add a glass of Milk
it's a meal I'm lovin'

Chiliburger hot
and French Fries too
an excellent meal
for me and you

Mayonnaise
is the latest craze
slather it on
you can't go wrong

Tacos really
hit the spot
especially when served
with Salsa, hot

A Pepperoni Pizza
also hits the spot
especially when it's hot...
or not...

I ate a Pear
an Orange and a Strawberry
then I had an Apple
was I happy? Very...

Eat more Twinkies
and people will speak
of your mastodonic
physique

A Bean and Cheese Burrito
is oh so sweet-o

A Chocolate Milkshake
is creamy deliciousness
I had one yesterday
The bonus? Nutritiousness

Fried Chicken with Gravy
is oh so good
I'd have some now
if I could

On a plate
Risotto
like lava
should flow

A Juicy Steak
can't be beat
add some Steak Sauce
I do like to eat

A Baked Potato
with Butter and Sour Cream
served piping hot
of that I dream...

Carne Asada
with Rice and Beans
and Spicy Salsa
my plate I cleans

5 Onion Soup
has 5 Onions in it
with Cheese on top
it's always a hit

A Hot Fudge Sundae
so sweet and gooey
I'll eat half
and save half for youey

Spaghetti and Meatballs
with Garlic Bread
a Crispy Salad
and I'm well fed

Cereal with Milk
is a tasty treat
all day long
it can't be beat

No one likes Brownies
I heard someone say
that's not true, I do
so send them my way

Prime Rib
and Horseradish
makes me oh
so very gladdish

Hot Chocolate soothes
a weary mind
at the end of the day
it's simply sublime

A Baloney Sandwich

_____

_____

_____

Mac and Cheese

_____

_____

_____

A Popsicle

_____

_____

_____

Watermelon

_____

_____

_____

THE END

ABOUT THE AUTHOR

Rusty Austin began his career writing book and movie reviews at his community college newspaper, The Rapp Street Journal, where he eventually became editor in chief. He moved on to graduate from UCLA Film School and then to Hollywood where he worked for many years as a TV producer. Along the way he discovered a talent for writing poetry. As his Hollywood career wound down he wrote a series of Facebook posts which gradually morphed into a large number of kid friendly and adult savvy poems. He has always had a soft spot for animals and food, so that's what he writes poems about! At the urging of his Facebook family, he turned those posts into books. His books always include a short DIY section to encourage kids to write their own poems and draw their own animals or favorite foods.

Also by Rusty
The Two-Headed Snake
The Unicorn Has One Horn
Beware the Grizzly Bear
The Carrot Is Orange

www.ingramcontent.com/pod-product-compliance
Lightning Source LLC
Chambersburg PA
CBHW041127120626
46547CB00019B/2893